Measuring Tim

Clocks and Calendars

Tracey Steffora

www.raintreepublishers.co.uk
Visit our website to find out
more information about
Raintree books.

To order:
☎ Phone 0845 6044371
🖷 Fax +44 (0) 1865 312263
🖳 Email myorders@raintreepublishers.co.uk

Customers from outside the UK please telephone +44 1865 312262

Raintree is an imprint of Capstone Global Library Limited, a company incorporated in England and Wales having its registered office at 7 Pilgrim Street, London, EC4V 6LB – Registered company number: 6695582

Edited by Tracey Steffora, Dan, Nunn and Sian Smith
Designed by Richard Parker
Picture research by Hannah Taylor
Originated by Capstone Global Library Ltd
Printed and bound in China by Leo Paper Products Ltd

ISBN 978 1 406 22304 0 (hardback)
15 14 13 12 11
10 9 8 7 6 5 4 3 2 1

ISBN 978 1 406 22311 8 (paperback)
16 15 14 13 12
10 9 8 7 6 5 4 3 2 1

British Library Cataloguing in Publication Data
Steffora, Tracey.
    Clocks and calendars. -- (Measuring time)
    1. Clocks and watches--Juvenile literature. 2. Calendars--Juvenile literature. 3. Time--Juvenile literature.
    I. Title II. Series
    529.3-dc22

Acknowledgements
We would like to thank the following for permission to reproduce photographs: Alamy Images pp. 5 (©STOCK4B GmbH), 14 (©Ian Shaw), 16 (©Jeannie Burleson), 19 (©Lourens Smak); Corbis p. 18 (Stefanie Grewel); Getty Images pp. 12 (Fuse), 17 (Gen Nishino); istockphoto pp. 4 (©Inga Ivanova), 8 (©Håkan Dahlström), **23 mid** (©Håkan Dahlström); Shutterstock pp. 6 (©Danila Bolshakov), 7 (©Lorraine Kourafas), 9 (©Hubenov), 10 (©Adrian Reynolds), **11** (©Yampi), 13 (©Sebos), 20 (©Blaz Kune), 21 (©Mariusz Szachowski).

Front cover photograph of calendar and alarm clock reproduced with permission of istockphoto (©Pali Rao). Back cover photograph of a sundial reproduced with permission of Shutterstock (© Hubenov).

Every effort has been made to contact copyright holders of any material reproduced in this book. Any omissions will be rectified in subsequent printings if notice is given to the publisher.

Contents

What is time?

Time is how long something takes.

Time is when things happen.

clock

calendar

Clocks and calendars help us to know when things happen.

Clocks

Clocks measure short amounts of time. A clock can show minutes and hours.

6

This clock is digital.

It shows 7 o'clock.

minute hand

hour hand

This clock has hands.

It shows 2 o'clock.

sundial

This clock uses the Sun to tell time.
It shows 2 o'clock.

Clocks can be large or small.

Clocks can be found in different places.

Calendars

Calendars measure longer times.
A calendar can show a day or
a week.

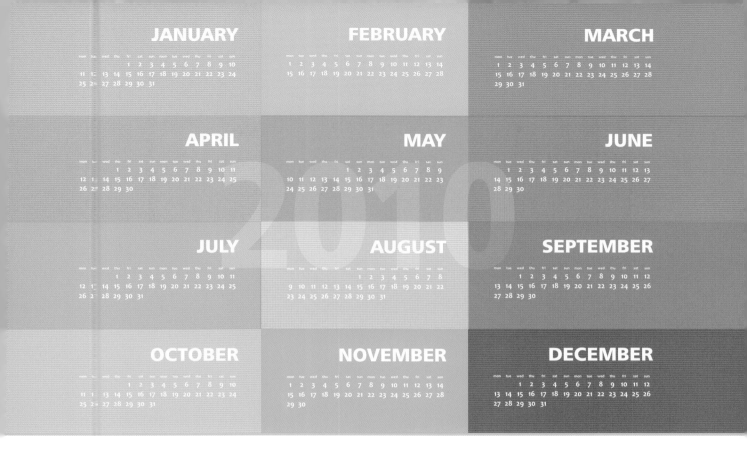

A calendar can show a month or a year.

A calendar can show us the weather.

AUGUST						
Sunday	Monday	Tuesday	Wednesday	Thursday	Friday	Saturday
	1	2	3	4	5	6 ◖
7	8	9	10	11	12	13 ○
14	15	16	17	18 ◗	19	20
21	22	23	24	25 ●	26	27
28	29	30	31			

◖ half moon   ○ full moon   ● new moon

A calendar can tell us what the Moon will look like.

15

A calendar can help us count the days we are in school.

A calendar can help us remember special days.

A calendar can hang on the wall.

A calendar can be on a computer.

Clocks and calendars

Clocks and calendars help us know what will happen today.

Clocks and calendars help us plan tomorrow.

Dates

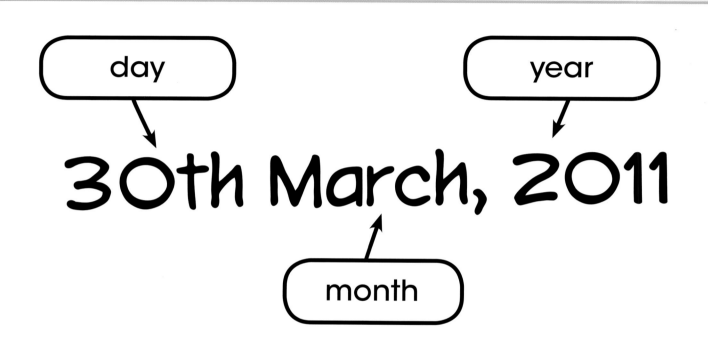

A date is a way we write time.
We write the day, month, and year.

Picture glossary

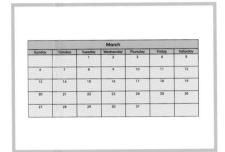

month one of the 12 parts of a year. A month is usually 30 or 31 days long.

o'clock a time of the day when the minute hand is pointing directly on the 12

23

Index

Notes for parents and teachers
Before reading
Counting and understanding numbers up to 60 is an important skill for children to master before they are able to understand how these numbers function on a clock and a calendar. Spend some time reviewing the concept of hours, minutes, and seconds with children, and discuss instances in which they use each unit to measure different events. Do the same with days, weeks, and months.

After reading
Review and discuss the different forms that clocks and calendars can take. Ask children to go on a clock and calendar hunt. This can be an individual activity and children can make a chart of where they find clocks and calendars. Or, make it a class activity and bring a digital camera along to record images of clocks and calendars, then use the images to construct a visual chart with the children.